Novel Unit Resources for
The Graveyard Book by Neil Gaiman

Resources created and compiled by
Sarah Pennington

All quoted text within from:

Gaiman, Neil. *The Graveyard Book*. New York: Harper Collins Publishers, 2008.

Table of Contents:

Common Core Anchor Standards for English Language Arts (Grades 6-12) Covered in This Novel Unit

Reading:

1. Read closely to determine what the text says explicitly and to make logical inferences from it; cite specific textual evidence when writing or speaking to support conclusions drawn from the text.

2. Determine central ideas or themes of a text and analyze their development; summarize the key supporting details and ideas.

3. Analyze how and why individuals, events, and ideas develop and interact over the course of a text.

4. Interpret words and phrases as they are used in a text, including determining technical, connotative, and figurative meanings, and analyze how specific word choices shape meaning or tone.

5. Analyze the structure of texts, including how specific sentences, paragraphs, and larger portions of the text (e.g., a section, chapter, scene, or stanza) relate to each other and the whole.

8. Delineate and evaluate the argument and specific claims in a text, including the validity of the reasoning as well as the relevance and sufficiency of the evidence.

Writing:

1. Write arguments to support claims in an analysis of substantive topics or texts, using valid reasoning and relevant and sufficient evidence.

3. Write narratives to develop real or imagined experiences or events using effective technique, well-chosen details, and well-structured event sequences.

7. Conduct short as well as more sustained research projects based on focused questions, demonstrating understanding of the subject under investigation.

8. Gather relevant information from multiple print and digital sources, assess the credibility and accuracy of each source, and integrate the information while avoiding plagiarism.

10. Write routinely over extended time frames (time for research, reflection, and revision) and shorter time frames (a single sitting or a day or two) for a range of tasks, purposes, and audiences.

Speaking & Listening:

1. Prepare for and participate effectively in a range of conversations and collaborations with diverse partners, building on others' ideas and expressing their own clearly and persuasively.

4. Present information, findings, and supporting evidence such that listeners can follow the line of reasoning and the organization, development, and style are appropriate to task, purpose, and audience.

Language:

4. Determine or clarify the meaning of unknown and multiple-meaning words and phrases by using context clues, analyzing meaningful word parts, and consulting general and specialized reference materials, as appropriate.

5. Demonstrate understanding of word relationships and nuances in word meanings.

6. Acquire and use accurately a range of general academic and domain-specific words and phrases sufficient for reading, writing, speaking, and listening at the college and career readiness level; demonstrate independence in gathering vocabulary knowledge when considering a word or phrase important to comprehension or expression.

Chapter 1

Vocabulary:

Obelisk (N): a four-sided tower of stone that tapers to a point. (Example: The Washington Monument is an obelisk.)

Obduracy (N): the state of being unmoved by persuasion; stubborn.

Discarnate (adj): without a physical body

Revenants (N): ghosts

Wights (N): ghosts

Luminescence (N): a soft glow not caused by an outside source

Masticating (V): chewing

Vocabulary practice ideas:
Write a poem!
Draw the meanings!
Create riddles!
Look up the etymology!
Sort by part of speech!

Comprehension Questions:

1. What is the job Jack has come to the house to complete?
2. How old is the child at the beginning of this story?
3. What happens that causes Mrs. Owens to take responsibility for the child?
4. What does the stranger convince Jack he had seen in the cemetery?
5. How does the child get the name "Nobody Owens?"
6. Who convinces the residents of the graveyard to give Nobody the "Freedom of the Graveyard?"

Extension/Discussion Questions:

1. How does the author set the tone of the story in this first chapter? Give details from the story that help to set this tone.
2. Who do you think the Lady on the Grey is?
3. How does Silas begin protecting Nobody even before agreeing to be his guardian?

Activity: Shuddering Synonyms

To prepare for this activity, have students write a short narrative (or pull a previously written sample). As a class, discuss Gaiman's use of synonyms for the word "ghost." How would the chapter be different if the author had just used the word "ghost" every time?

Now have students complete the activitiy. Each student will choose four words from his/her own writing and find three synonyms for each word. (This can be done on the included worksheet.)

After students complete the activity, give them an opportunity to rewrite their narrative using some of the synonyms to make it more interesting.

Possible topics for student narrative:

How three ducks got lost in the graveyard

Why the Lady on the Grey chose to help Nobody

What the man Jack does to try and locate the baby after chapter 1 ends

Shuddering Synonyms

In chapter 1, the author uses a variety of words that mean "ghost." Would the chapter have been as interesting to read without these synonyms?

Choose four words from your own writing and, using a thesaurus, find three synonyms for each of your words.

Now rewrite your narrative using some of the synonyms you found to make your story more interesting to read!

Chapter 2

Vocabulary:

Anorak (N): a pullover jacket or coat with a hood originally worn in polar regions.

Barrow (N): a hill or mound of earth used as a tomb or grave.

Brooch (N): a decorative pin, often large, used to close a cloak or for decoration

Comprehension Questions:

1. Who answers Nobody's questions in a way he can understand?
2. What skills does Nobody gain because he has the Freedom of the Graveyard?
3. How does Silas make learning the alphabet a game for Nobody?
4. Describe Nobody's first friend from outside the graveyard.
5. What do Scarlett's parents think of her new friend?
6. Who is the oldest active resident of the graveyard?
7. Where does Nobody take Scarlett in an attempt to win back her friendship?
8. What do Scarlett & Bod see in the Barrow?
9. What is the biggest consequence of Bod & Scarlett's adventure?

Extension/Discussion Questions:

1. Why do you think Scarlett is able to see Bod?
2. The Sleer say that fear is a weapon. Do you agree? Explain why or why not.
3. Bod observes that "The treasures of ten thousand years ago were not the treasures of today." Is this true? Explain your response.
4. Scarlett tells Bod he is the bravest person she knows. Do you agree?

Chapter 3

Vocabulary:

Ghoul (N): an evil spirit or monster which eats the flesh of dead creatures.

Abandonment (N): the state of being left completely

Offal (N): garbage; useless left-over bits of something

Piebald (adj): having patches of black and white or other colors on the skin

Comprehension Questions:

1. What event upsets Bod in the beginning of this chapter?

2. Who does Silas bring to take care of Bod while he is away?

3. Besides bringing Bod food, what else does Bod feel Silas does for him?

4. Describe Miss Lupescu's lessons.

5. Describe the three creatures Bod meets when he wakes up.

6. How does Bod escape the ghouls?

7. The night-gaunts saved Bod three times. List how they saved him.

8. What sort of creature is Miss Lupescu?

9. Based on the gift he brings Bod, where has Silas been on his trip?

Extension/Discussion Questions:

1. The beginning of chapter 3 is an excellent opportunity to discuss <u>foreshadowing</u>. Why does the author choose this point in the story to introduce the idea of a ghoul-gate? How might this be important to know?

2. The ghouls say that they are more important than any people, even kings or queens, "in the same way that people are more important than Brussels sprouts." What do they mean by this statement? Do you agree?

3. Why does Bod feel stupid as he is being carried by the ghouls toward Ghulheim?

4. Why do you think the relationship between Bod and Miss Lupescu changes after she saves him from the ghouls?

Activity: Exploring Languages

In this chapter, Nobody is taught how to call for help in a variety of languages. Ask students to do the following: Choose a useful phrase or sentence and find out how to say it in at least four languages you do not know. (This can be done using a variety of web sites, including Google translate.)

Possible phrases/sentences:

Where is the restroom?	I am thirsty.
I am lost.	What time is it?
Where am I?	

Chapter 4

Vocabulary:

Hasten (V): speed up

Unshriven (adj): without one's sins forgiven or confession heard

Promiscuous (adj): all mingled together without any order

Lummox (N): a clumsy, foolish person

Comprehension Questions:

1. What is Slipping and Fading and why would these be important skills for Bod to know?

2. What lessons does Bod receive from Miss Letitia Borrows & why does Bod like her?

3. How does Bod end up in the Potter's Field?

4. Who is Liza Hempstock?

5. How has Bod collected most of the money he has?

6. How much money does Bod have?

7. Why does Bod take the brooch from the barrow?

8. Where does Bod find clothes to wear into the outside world?

9. Describe Abanazer Bolger.

10. Abanazer Bolger tells Hustings that he has two kinds of treasure. What are they?

11. Who saves Bod from the men in the shop and how does she do it?

12. Does Nobody succeed in his quest for Liza?

Extension/Discussion Questions:

1. Are the Sleer effective guardians? Explain.

2. Why is Abanazer so careful in questioning Bod about where he got the brooch? What does this tell you about Abanazer's character?

3. Why do you think the black-edged card only has the name Jack on it and no other information?

Additional Activities:

1. Mr. Pennyworth's description of Bod's Fading (involving the lion, elephant, and unicorn) can be seen as an example of a hyperbole. (A purposeful exaggeration often made to stress a point.) This is a good opportunity to discuss hyperbole and give commonly used examples. The lesson can be wrapped up by asking students to write their own lengthy hyperbole, using Mr. Pennyworth's as an example.

2. How much money does Bod have? Have students look up what Bod's two pounds and fifty pence is worth in U.S. currency.

Chapter 5

Vocabulary:

Danse Macabre (N): French; dance of death

Comprehension Questions:

1. What important items does Silas bring Nobody in this chapter?

2. How long has it been since the winter flowers bloomed and everyone danced the Macabray?

3. Why does Silas not dance the Macabray?

4. What distracts Bod from the questions he wants to ask Silas?

Extension/Discussion Questions:

1. The Lady Mayoress doesn't understand why she must cut and distribute the winter flowers, but her companions insist it is a tradition. Does anyone truly understand why this tradition is followed? Explain.

2. After the Macabray, Josiah Worthington tells Bod that he is not one of them (the dead). This is the first time Bod has seen himself as being apart from his friends and family. How do you think this will affect Bod?

3. The *danse macabre* (mispronounced by the characters in this book as Macabray) is an ancient theme in art which promotes the idea that all are equal in death. Do you agree with this idea? Explain.

Interlude

Comprehension Questions:

1. What is the only thing all the men in the Washington Room have in common?

2. What is the man on stage sharing with the group?

3. Who tells the man Jack he is out of time and on a deadline?

Extension/Discussion Questions:

1. Who else might have been involved in the "trouble in San Francisco" that the man Jack mentions?

2. Now that Jack has been given a deadline, how do you think his approach to the problem will change?

The interlude is a great time to stop and review what has happened and make some predictions about the remainder of the book. Will Jack Frost find Nobody? How? What will happen when/if he does?

Create a character map of Nobody at this point in the story, then create another at the end of the story and use the two to see how Nobody has changed. This is a great assignment for students to put into a reading journal, and can grow into an essay assignment in which the student discuss how and why Nobody changed as he did within the story.

Chapter 6

Vocabulary:

Apoplexy (N): a stroke; a sudden loss of body function due to a collapsed blood vessel

Pell-mell (adv): in a hurried and reckless manner, quickly & without caution

Comprehension Questions:

1. What book is Nobody reading at the beginning of this chapter and to whom does it belong?

2. Who tells Bod that Silas is looking for him?

3. What does Silas share with Nobody that he hadn't been told before?

4. What does Silas say that Nobody has that the dead do not?

5. Why does Bod want to go to school?

6. Describe Nick Farthing & Maureen Quilling.

7. How does Bod make himself a target for Nick & Mo?

8. How does Bod deal with Nick & Mo?

9. Who does Bod meet in the small graveyard after Nick & Mo run away?

10. What does Bod learn about Silas from the Perssons?

11. How does school change for Bod after he scares Nick & Mo?

12. How does Bod deal with Nick and what does he discover about Nick that he can use against him?

13. Who convinces Bod not to run away?

14. Who lies to the police and gets Bod arrested?

15. Why isn't Bod able to Fade when he is cornered by the police?

16. How does Bod escape from the police?

17. How does Bod get revenge on Mo?

Extension/Discussion Questions:

1. Thackaray Porringer dies due to his own anger at having a practical joke played on him. Have you ever played a joke on someone that turned out badly? Have you ever been the target of a joke that you didn't think was funny?

2. When told that there is a man out in the world who wants to kill him, Bod is not concerned. How has being raised in the graveyard made Nobody's perception of death different from that of "normal" boys his age?

3. Nobody tells Silas that the question to ask when it comes to the man who killed his family is "who will keep him safe from me?" How could Nobody be a threat to the man Jack?

4. In this chapter, the statement is made that "Fear is contagious." Do you agree?

Chapter 7

Vocabulary:

Imposition (N): a burden or obligation

Cached (V): concealed or hidden

Quadrant (N): a section that is about 1/4 of a full area

Unction (N): an ointment or healing salve

Balm (N): an ointment or healing salve

Propitious (adj): favorable

Doggerel (N): poor, of low quality

Approbation (N): approval

Posterity (N): future generations

Implacable (adj): unbending; showing no weakness

Incongruous (adj): out of place; inappropriate

Dominions (N): lands or countries ruled by a king or other ruler

Firmament (N): the sky

Juddered (V): vibrated violently

Providence (N): foresight; events planned in advance by a greater power

Snare (N): a type of drum

(N): a trap

Susurrus (N): whisper

Comprehension Questions:

1. What has Mr. & Mrs. Owens and Josiah Worthington so worried at the beginning of this chapter?

2. Who returns to the graveyard after a long absence?

3. How does Scarlett meet Mr. Frost?

4. How does Scarlett get home from the graveyard on the evening she takes the wrong bus?

5. What does Scarlett mention that upsets her mother?

6. Where does Scarlett first see Bod when she returns to the town?

7. To whom does Bod go for advice on how to approach Scarlett?

8. When Bod sees Scarlett again, what does she ask permission to do?

9. Where are Silas and Miss Lupescu when we first see them in this chapter?

10. Why does Scarlett get upset with Bod when he is telling her about his past and his family?

11. Who does Scarlett enlist to help her find more information about Bod and his murdered family?

12. What does Scarlett discover when she looks in the old newspapers at the library?

13. Although no battles are shown between Silas's team and any opponents, it is clear that battle is occurring. What are some of the clues the author gives to show us that the battle is happening and that it is a difficult fight?

14. Mr. Frost calls Scarlett on Sunday afternoon with news. What does he have to share with her.

15. Bod finally decides to go ask the oldest thing in the graveyard for advice. Name this thing.

16. What does the Sleer want and what will it do once it has it?

17. What does the Sleer advise Bod to do?

18. Who is Mr. Frost?

19. What does Mr. Frost want to show Bod when he takes him upstairs?

20. How does Bod escape Mr. Frost?

21. Who knocks at Mr. Frost's door?

22. Where does Bod hide Scarlett?

23. Why is it important that Jack Ketch's black cord is strong and invisible to X-rays?

24. How does Bod deal with Jack Ketch?

25. Who tells Bod why the Jacks want to kill him?

26. Why do the Jacks want Bod dead?

27. How does Bod get rid of three of the Jacks at once?

28. How does Bod get rid of Jack Frost?

29. How does Scarlett feel about Bod after he saves her?

30. What happens to Scarlett after Bod saves her from Mr. Frost?

31. What happened to Miss Lupescu?

32. Where does Silas take Nobody after telling him about Miss Lupescu?

Extension/Discussion Questions:

1. Bod has begun to outgrow some of his friends at the graveyard. Explain how this is happening.

2. Master Trot tells Nobody about his plot for revenge against a critic of his poems. Do you think that Trot actually got his revenge? Does it matter if he actually got revenge as long as he is satisfied?

3. Silas is travelling with Miss Luprescu (a werewolf), Haroun (an Ifrit or fire spirit/genie) and Kandar (a mummy) and they are engaged in hunting down some sort of creatures. What might unite these four and cause them to fight together?

4. When Mr. Dandy discovers that Bod has escaped again, he says "Once is a mistake, Jack. Twice is a disaster." Does this statement apply to any situations in real life?

5. How is the Jacks of All Trades' reason for killing Nobody's family ironic?

6. Even when he is about to close them in the ghoul gate, Bod still gives Mr. Dandy tips on surviving once he is through. What does this tell you about Bod as a person?

7. Why do you think Jack Frost is able to hear the Sleer?

8. How do you feel about Silas's decision to make Scarlett forget about Bod? Was it the right choice? Explain.

Activities:

1. Jack Who? The various Jacks all have last names that are references to different characters and/or people. Using the included worksheet, have students research each Jack's name to find its original meaning.

Jack Who?

Each member of the Jacks of All Trades has a last name that is a reference to another person or character in history or literature. Research to find out what each Jack's name refers to.

Jack name:	Origin or meaning:
Jack of All Trades	
Jack Tar	
Jack Dandy (Jack-a-dandy)	
Jack Nimble	
Jack Ketch	
Jack Frost	

Chapter 8

Vocabulary:

Discomfited (V): confused; disconcerted
Wrong-footed (adj): confused, off-balance

Comprehension Questions:

1. What is happening to Bod at the beginning of this chapter?

2. How does Bod injure his head?

3. What is the only visible writing left on Mother Slaughter's headstone?

4. How is Mother Slaughter's memory of Nobody's arrival in the graveyard different from the way it actually happened?

5. Why are Bod's parents waiting for him next to their tomb?

6. Why is Silas packed up?

7. What does Silas tell Nobody the Honour Guard does?

8. What does Silas give Nobody to help him start out in the world?

9. Who is the last resident of the graveyard Nobody sees before leaving?

Extension/Discussion Questions:

1. In chapter 8, the author says, "The world was changing." Do you agree that the world is changing in this story, or is it something else?

Final Essay Topic Ideas for *The Graveyard Book*

- Nobody Owens goes from being an orphan to having a new family in a single night. How does his "non-traditional" family life affect Nobody's interactions with others throughout the novel?

- Nobody is saved from Jack that first night by the love of two mothers. Compare and contrast the sacrifices of both of Nobody's mothers.

- At the end of the story, Scarlett sees Nobody as a monster. Is he a monster? Defend your position with examples from the story.

- Choose one of the following themes and write how it applies to *The Graveyard Book* and what the novel could be specifically saying about your chosen theme.
  Courage
  Friendship
  Family & Community
  Change
  Death
  Learning & Education
  Good versus Evil

- Silas states at the end of the book that he used to be a monster but that he changed. Has he really changed? Support your response with examples from the story.

Additional During Reading Activity Suggestions:

- Before beginning each chapter, give students the name of the chapter and have them make predictions about the events of the chapter based on the title. After reading the chapter, have them look over their predictions and discuss.
- Have students create a conflict chart as they read the story. For each chapter, ask students to list one or two major conflicts in that chapter and to tell whether each conflict is internal or external.
- Have students choose a favorite scene and turn it into a reader's theater script to perform for the class. This is a great way to gauge understanding and to allow them to have fun with the story.
- As students read, have them create a chart with examples of figurative language (metaphor, simile, personification, onomatopoeia, etc.) listing the example, what form of figurative language it is, and the page on which it can be found. This can be done individually, in small groups on chart paper, or on a bulletin board as a whole class activity.
- Have students create a plot chart as they read, charting where the major events of the story fit. (The climax would be the showdown between Bod & Jack Frost in the Barrow.)

After Reading Wrap-Up Project/Activity Suggestions:

- Have students create a newspaper about the events in the novel. The newspaper can include a main article (summary of the novel), a human interest story (a character sketch of one of the characters and his/her role in the story), an advice column (what advice would one of the characters ask for and what would the student tell him/her?) and advertisements (what products might characters in the story need or want?)
- Create a talk show featuring characters from the story. Students can take the roles of the various characters and get "interviewed" by the talk show host about the events of the story and how they felt about the outcome.
- Write a series of diary entries (3-4) from the perspective of a character other than Nobody. How did that character feel about the events that were taking place during the story? Did he/she know and understand what was happening? Explain.
- Write a letter to the author of the book. What would you like to tell him/her? Did you enjoy the book? Why or why not? What would you like to know that the book didn't quite tell you? Would you like to read more about the characters?
- Write a poem or rap summarizing the major events of the book.
- Create a resume for one of the characters in the novel. What are his/her skills? Accomplishments? Goals?

Full Vocabulary List for *The Graveyard Book* *(Chapter number in parenthesis)*

Abandonment (N): the state of being left completely (3)

Anorak (N): a pullover jacket or coat with a hood originally worn in polar regions. (2)

Apoplexy (N): a stroke; a sudden loss of body function due to a collapsed blood vessel (6)

Approbation (N): approval (7)

Balm (N): an ointment or healing salve (7)

Barrow (N): a hill or mound of earth used as a tomb or grave. (2)

Brooch (N): a decorative pin, often large, used to close a cloak or for decoration (2)

Cached (V): concealed or hidden (7)

Danse Macabre (N): French; dance of death (5)

Discarnate (adj): without a physical body (1)

Discomfited (V): confused; disconcerted (8)

Dominions (N): lands or countries ruled by a king or other ruler (7)

Doggerel (N): poor, of low quality (7)

Firmament (N): the sky (7)

Ghoul (N): an evil spirit or monster which eats the flesh of dead creatures. (3)

Hasten (V): speed up (4)

Implacable (adj): unbending; showing no weakness (7)

Imposition (N): a burden or obligation (7)

Incongruous (adj): out of place; inappropriate (7)

Juddered (V): vibrated violently (7)

Luminescence (N): a soft glow not caused by an outside source (1)

Lummox (N): a clumsy, foolish person (4)

Masticating (V): chewing (1)

Obduracy (N): the state of being unmoved by persuasion; stubborn.(1)

Obelisk (N): a four-sided tower of stone that tapers to a point. (Example: The Washington Monument is an obelisk.) (1)

Offal (N): garbage; useless left-over bits of something (3)

Pell-mell (adv): in a hurried and reckless manner, quickly & without caution (6)

Piebald (adj): having patches of black and white or other colors on the skin (3)

Posterity (N): future generations (7)

Promiscuous (adj): all mingled together without any order (4)

Propitious (adj): favorable (7)

Providence (N): foresight; events planned in advance by a greater power (7)

Quadrant (N): a section that is about 1/4 of a full area (7)

Revenants (N): ghosts (1)

Snare (N): a type of drum (7)
        (N): a trap (7)

Susurrus (N): whisper (7)

Unction (N): an ointment or healing salve (7)

Unshriven (adj): without one's sins forgiven or confession heard (4)

Wights (N): ghosts (1)

Wrong-footed (adj): confused, off-balance (8)

Comprehension & Extension/Discussion Question Answer Keys:

Chapter 1 Comprehension Question Answers:

1. He has come to kill the family that lives there.
2. The child is one and a half years old.
3. The ghost of the child's mother asks her to protect her child.
4. The stranger convinces Jack that what he saw was a fox.
5. Mrs. Owens says, "He looks like nobody but himself," so Silas decides that Nobody is a good name, and Owens is the last name of the ghosts who take him in.
6. The Lady on the Grey convinces the residents to let Nobody stay .

Chapter 1 Extension/Discussion Question Answers:

1. Answers will vary, but may contain the following:
   The dark tone of the story is set by details such as: repetition of words such as darkness, the man's knife, fog, the chilly breeze, etc.
2. Answers may vary, but may include the idea that she is a representation of death since it says that "each one of us encounters the Lady on the Grey at the end of our days."
3. Silas uses his powers to confuse Jack and send him away from the graveyard, forgetting that he ever saw the child there.

Chapter 2 Comprehension Question Answers:

1. Silas answers Bod's questions.
2. Because he has Freedom of the Graveyard, Nobody can see in the dark, travel in ways that most living people cannot, and living people do not notice him.
3. Silas gives Nobody a "quest" to find all the letters of the alphabet within the graveyard.
4. Nobody's first friend from outside the graveyard is a girl named Scarlett Amber Perkins who is five years old.
5. Scarlett's parents believe that Nobody is Scarlett's imaginary friend.
6. Caius Pompeius is the oldest active resident of the graveyard.
7. He takes her into a barrow, which is the oldest grave in the cemetery. No one knows who is buried there.
8. In the Barrow, Scarlett & Bod see a large man covered with indigo ink or tattoos.
9. The biggest consequence of their adventure is that Scarlet is not allowed to wander the graveyard out of sight of her parents anymore and only comes back one time to say good-bye to Nobody before the family moves to Scotland.

Chapter 2 Extension/Discussion Question Answers:

1. Answers may vary. Possible answers may take into account Scarlett's age and innocence, the fact that she may not be seen as a threat to Bod, or that Bod wants a friend and that desire makes him seen by the most likely prospect.
2. Answers will vary.
3. Answers will vary, but students may make points such as:
   People in different times will have differing perspectives on value
   Things may become outdated and, therefore, unimportant with the passage of time

Things that had no value may be more valuable now because they are rare

4. Answers will vary. Some students may agree based on the fact that Bod stood up to the Indigo Man & the Sleer. Others may disagree for various reasons, including the fact that Bod has never truly known danger, having been kept safe for as long as he can remember.

Chapter 3 Comprehension Question Answers:

1. Silas is leaving.
2. Silas brings a woman named Miss Lupescu to care for Bod while he is gone.
3. Bod looks to Silas to give him advice, tell him about the world outside, and make him feel safe.
4. Miss Lupescu's lessons are boring to Bod and consist of memorizing and reciting lists. The lists are always printed in pale purple ink and smell strange.
5. The three creatures Bod meets when he wakes up are just a little bigger than he is, and look like mummies. They have sharp teeth and beady eyes and claws on their fingers. The biggest of the three is the Duke of Westminster. The Bishop of Bath & Wells has a very long tongue and piebald skin, and Harchibald Fitzhugh is the third.
6. Bod's escape starts when he finds a screw in the bag where he is trapped and begins to tear holes in the bag with it. He stops when he sees a large dog-like creature outside. The creature tears the bag open and the ghouls run away, leaving Bod behind. Bod tries to escape the creature, but twists his ankle and falls down the steps, where he is caught by a night-gaunt which returns him to the dog, who turns out to be Miss Lupescu.
7. The night-gaunts saved Bod by: letting Miss Lupescu know where he was, by getting rid of the ghouls who wanted to kill Bod, and by catching him as he was falling off the stairs.
8. Miss Lupescu is a Hound of God, which is what werewolves call themselves.
9. Based on the gift, Silas has been to San Francisco.

Chapter 3 Extension/Discussion Question Answers:

1. Students may respond that a ghoul-gate will become important in this chapter and may make predictions regarding how it will become so.
2. The ghouls feel they are more important because they eat the kings, queens, etc. just like people eat Brussels sprouts, and that this means they are more important or better than people. Students responses will vary regarding the second question.
3. Answers will vary, but may include the following:
   Bod knows that he has put himself in danger and should have known better.
   If Bod had been paying better attention to his lesson with Miss Lupescu, he might have realized earlier what the creatures were and escaped.
4. Answers may vary, but may include: Bod & Miss Lupescu's relationship changes after she saves him from the ghouls because they now have a shared experience that has helped Bod to realize that Miss Lupescu does care for him, now Bod knows who/what Miss Lupescu really is and understands her better, etc.

Chapter 4 Comprehension Question Answers:

1. Slipping is the ability to "slip through shadows" and Fading is to "fade from awareness." These could be important because they let Bod travel unnoticed and safe.
2. Miss Letitia Borrows teaches Bod grammar and composition. He likes her because her crypt is cozy and she is easily led off-topic.
3. Bod is trying to get the last apple out of the apple tree when the branch breaks and drops him in the compost pile in the Potter's Field.
4. Liza Hempstock is the witch buried in the Potter's Field. She was drowned and then burned, but managed to curse all who were present before she died. She was buried with no headstone to mark her resting place.
5. Bod has collected money mostly by searching an area after it has been used by a young couple for snuggling and kissing.
6. Bod has two pounds and fifty-three pence.
7. Bod takes the brooch because he hopes to use it (or sell it) to get a headstone for Liza.
8. Bod finds clothes in the gardener's shed.
9. Abanazer Bolger owns a shop and is not an honest person. He always looks unhappy and uses this expression to cheat people by paying them less than what the items they want to sell are worth.
10. The first treasure is the brooch itself. Abanazer hopes that Nobody will lead him to the barrow and that it will be filled with more items like the brooch. The second treasure is Nobody; Abanazer remembers that the man Jack was looking for a boy and realizes that Nobody could be the right one.
11. Liza saves Bod by first helping him become able to Fade and then (as some students may infer) by tricking the men into fighting among themselves until both are unconscious.
12. Nobody does succeed, He uses the glass paperweight he took from the shop and paints Liza's initials on it, along with "we don't forget," then places it where he thinks her head would be.

Chapter 4 Extension/Discussion Question Answers:

1. Answers will vary. Some will say yes, since no one has managed to take any of the items before this, and some have been scared away or even scared to death by the Sleer. Others may disagree since Bod was able to take something and walk right out with it, despite the fear caused by the Sleer.
2. Abanazer wants to be sure that the brooch hasn't been stolen from someone who will come looking for it. He doesn't want trouble. This shows that he is cautious in his business dealings and doesn't like too much attention.
3. Answers will vary, but students may say that the card is magical and can be used to call Jack and reach him wherever he may be. It clearly has some connection to him, since he can sense that something has happened after Nobody takes the card.

Chapter 5 Comprehension Question Answers:

1. Silas brings Nobody clothes so that he can get used to wearing them and can blend in if he needs to.
2. It has been 80 years since the last time the winter flowers loomed and everyone danced the Macabray.
3. Silas does not dance because he is neither living nor dead.
4. Bod is distracted from his questions by snow. This is only the third time he has seen it.

Chapter 5 Extension/Discussion Question Answers:

1. No living person truly understands the reason for the tradition because no one living remembers the event after it has happened and none of the dead will discuss it.
2. Answers may vary, but may include: Bod may begin to seek out others like himself now that he realizes he is different from the rest of the residents of the graveyard. He may start to spend more time in the outside world, even if everyone warns him not to.
3. Answers will vary.

Interlude Comprehension Question Answers:

1. The only thing the men have in common is their black suits.
2. He is announcing the "Good Deeds Done" by the group, including the purchase of kidney machines.
3. Mr. Dandy tells Jack he is on a deadline now.

Interlude Extension/Discussion Question Answers:

1. Silas might have been involved, since he was in San Francisco at the same time and when he came back, he appeared to be injured (his right arm).
2. Answers will vary.

Chapter 6 Comprehension Question Answers:

1. He is reading *Robinson Crusoe* and the book belongs to Thackeray Porringer.
2. Tom Sands tells Bod that Silas is looking for him.
3. Silas tells Nobody that he had parents and a sister who were killed and that the killer is still out there looking for Bod to kill him as well.
4. Silas tells Bod that he has potential, which is gone when one is dead.
5. Bod wants to go to school to learn about all the things in the outside world that he cannot in the graveyard.
6. Nick Farthing is a large boy who likes to shoplift and bully smaller kids. Maureen Quilling is a thin pale girl with blue eyes who tells Nick what to steal and who to bully.
7. Bod makes himself a target by advising the other students to stop paying Nick and Mo and telling them what to say to get the pair of bullies to leave them alone for good.
8. Bod leads Nick & Mo to a graveyard where he first Fades and then inflicts them with Fear so that they run away.
9. Bod meets the Persson family: Amabella, Roderick (Roddy), & Portunia.
10. Bod learns that Silas is a member of the Honour Guard.
11. School is different because people are noticing Bod now and he is not used to being noticed. Nick even stabs him in the hand with a pencil to show he isn't afraid of Bod.
12. Bod appears in Nick's dream and tells him to reform or else. He also finds out that Nick is afraid of spiders, which could turn out to be useful.
13. Liza convinces Bod not to run away from the graveyard.
14. Mo gets Bod arrested by saying that he was in her back garden breaking things.
15. Bod can't Fade because everybody's attention was focused on him.
16. Bod escapes when Silas intentionally gets hit by the police car. Bod says they hit his father and manages

to get the two policemen arguing with each other. While their attention is diverted, he & Silas Fade and return to the graveyard.

17. Bod gets revenge on Mo by appearing in the science lab as she is cleaning up and implying that he will haunt her before disappearing.

Chapter 6 Extension/Discussion Question Answers:

1. Answers will vary.
2. Answers will vary, but may point out that being raised by ghosts has made Bod less afraid of death, since he does not see it as being final. He does not understand the fear of losing someone to death as other children might because his friends and "parents" (Mr. & Mrs. Owens) are dead and still hanging around with no fear of them ever leaving the graveyard.
3. Answers will vary, but could include Nobody's ability to Fade and the knowledge he has gained from the residents of the graveyard.
4. Answers will vary.

Chapter 7 Comprehension Question Answers:

1. Silas has gone away and has not left anyone to care for Bod.
2. Scarlett returns when her parents split up. She gets on the wrong bus one day after school and ends up at the gates of the graveyard.
3. Scarlett meets Mr. Frost when she gets on the wrong bus and ends up at the graveyard where he is making rubbings of old stones.
4. Mr. Frost takes her home.
5. Scarlett's mother becomes upset when Scarlett mentions the graveyard.
6. Scarlett first sees Bod in her dream the night Mr. Frost brings her back from the graveyard.
7. Bod goes to Nehemiah Trot, a poet, for advice about Scarlett.
8. Scarlett asks Bod's permission to give him a hug.
9. Silas and Miss Lupescu are in Krakow in caves deep beneath Wawel Hill, even below the caves called the Dragon's Den.
10. Scarlett gets mad at Bod because he won't tell her about his guardian.
11. Scarlett asks Mr. Frost for help finding information about the murders.
12. Scarlett discovers that there was a murder, but that little was ever said about it, like it was swept under the rug. She also discovers that it took place in the house where Mr. Frost is staying.
13. We know that battle is happening and that it is a difficult fight for many reasons. Miss Lupescu is injured, with blood on her face (some of which is her own) and Silas is holding her because she has fallen. Kandar has a mangled wing which will never work properly again.
14. Mr. Frost says he has found more information about the murders, but he will only share it with Scarlett's friend.
15. The oldest thing in the graveyard is the Sleer.
16. The Sleer wants a new master and once it has a new master, it will hold him forever and keep him safe.
17. The Sleer tells Bod to find his name.
18. Mr. Frost is really Jack.
19. He doesn't want to show him anything – he wants to finish his job by killing Bod.

20. When Mr. Frost's attention is elsewhere, Bod Fades, sneaks out of the room, and locks Mr. Frost inside.

21. Four other Jacks knock at Mr. Frost's door, all dressed in black suits.

22. Bod hides Scarlett inside the hill (the barrow).

23. It is important because that means it is strong enough to do its job (kill people) and not seen as a weapon when Jack Ketch is travelling.

24. Bod tricks Ketch into jumping to attack him and falling into Mr. Carstairs's grave, twenty feet down, where he breaks his ankle.

25. Mr. Dandy tells him why the Jacks want him dead.

26. The Jacks want Bod dead because of a prophecy about a child who would be able to walk the border between the living and dead. In the prophecy, if this child were to live to be an adult, he would destroy the Jacks of All Trades. Bod is that child.

27. Bod opens up the ghoul gate and Jack Tar, Jack Nimble, and Jack Dandy fall in.

28. Bod tricks Jack Frost into becoming the new master of the Sleer, who then take him away with them to protect him.

29. Scarlett is afraid of Bod and calls him a monster because he knew what the Sleer would do to Jack Frost.

30. Silas takes her home and makes both her & her mother forget all about Nobody and they make plans to move back to Glasgow.

31. Miss Lupescu died fighting to protect others.

32. Silas takes Nobody to get pizza.

Chapter 7 Extension/Discussion Question Answers:

1. Bod is maturing and his interests are changing, but the ghosts are always the same age and they do not change at all. As Bod grows older, he becomes friends with ghosts who were closer to his own age when they died, but this means he is always leaving some old friends behind.

2. Answers will vary.

3. Answers will vary, but students may note that all are supernatural creatures, and that they may all be good, possibly misunderstood (based on their knowledge of Silas & Miss Lupescu), creatures fighting against some great evil.

4. Answers will vary.

5. The Jacks' reason for killing Nobody's family is ironic because their actions cause Nobody to gain the skills talked about in the prophecy, making him one who walks the border between life and death. Without their actions, the prophecy may never have come to pass.

6. Answers will vary, but may include: The fact that Nobody gives Mr. Dandy survival tips for beyond the ghoul gate shows that although Bod wants to be free of the Jacks, he isn't a killer like them. He is willing to give them a chance to have a life somewhere far away where they can no longer hurt him or anyone he cares about.

7. Answers will vary, but may include: Jack Frost can hear the Sleer because he has some magic abilities and these make him able to see things other people can't.

8. Answers will vary.

Chapter 8 Comprehension Question Answers:

1. Bod is losing some of the abilities that the Freedom of the Graveyard gave him.
2. Bod tries to peer into his friend Alonso's grave to see if he is there, but his head hits the ground instead of going through as it used to.
3. The only visible writing left on Mother Slaughter's headstone is LAUGH.
4. Mother Slaughter tells that she was all for letting Nobody stay in the graveyard and that the Lady on the Grey supported her in this, when actually Mother Slaughter was against him staying that night.
5. They are waiting to say good-bye to him because it is time for him to go.
6. Silas has packed up because he is no longer needed to be Bod's guardian, so he plans to return to his home.
7. Silas tells Nobody that the Honour Guard "protects the borders of things."
8. Silas gives Nobody a wallet with enough money to venture out into the world, a passport with his name on it, and a suitcase with his belongings in it.
9. The last graveyard resident Nobody sees is his mother, Mrs. Owens.

Chapter 8 Extension/Discussion Question Answers:

1. Answers will vary, but may include: The world is not changing in this story, but Nobody is. He is growing older and it is becoming time for him to go out and see the world on his own instead of listen to the stories of the graveyard residents. Now that he is almost grown up and the Jacks are gone, Bod can safely venture out into the world and no longer needs the protection of the graveyard.

Jack Who? (Answer Key)

Each member of the Jacks of All Trades has a last name that is a reference to another person or character in history or literature. Research to find out what each Jack's name refers to.

Jack name:	Origin or meaning:
Jack of All Trades	A Jack of All Trades is someone who is good at many different skills. The phrase usually ends "Master of None," implying that the skills are not outstanding in any area.
Jack Tar	A British term for a sailor in the Navy or merchant marine.
Jack Dandy (Jack-a-dandy)	A Jack-a-dandy is a term for someone who places great importance on their appearance and manner of dress (clothing).
Jack Nimble	From a nursery rhyme: Jack be nimble, Jack be quick, Jack jump over The candlestick.
Jack Ketch	Originally an English executioner who was known for the pain he inflicted on those to be executed. His name came to be used for death, Satan, and executioners in general.
Jack Frost	A personification of winter who, in stories, is responsible for bringing cold winds, frost, and snow.

Test Question Bank :

Character Questions:

Match each of the following characters with the description that best matches him/her.

A. Silas	B. Nobody Owens	C. The Lady on the Grey
D. Caius Pompeius	E. Mr. Frost	F. Scarlett Perkins

1. The living girl who befriends Nobody.

2. The oldest ghostly resident of the graveyard.

3. The main character of the story, he is an orphan being raised by ghosts.

4. The main character's protector, he is neither living nor dead.

5. The character who convinces the residents of the graveyard to let Nobody stay.

6. The man who searches for the main character in order to kill him, he pretends to be a historian.

Match each of the following characters with the description that best matches him/her.

A. Miss Lupescu	B. Mr. Dandy	C. Liza Hempstock
D. Abanazer Bolger	E. Nick Farthing	F. the Sleer

7. Another member of the Jacks of All Trades, he falls through a ghoul-gate.

8. A school bully who Nobody scares into being good.

9. The main character's secondary guardian who steps in when Silas has to travel.

10. A witch who was buried in the Potter's Field.

11. A creature that lives in the hill barrow at the graveyard.

12. A shopkeeper who tries to imprison Nobody and turn him over to Jack.

Story Questions:

1. The baby is taken in to be raised by:
   A. The Lady on the Grey
   B. Mr. & Mrs. Owens
   C. Mr. & Mrs. Caraway
   D. Miss Lupescu

2. This is the dance that the residents of the graveyard and the living people of the town dance together.
   A. Macabray
   B. Minuet
   C. Macarena
   D. Cha Cha

3. This person has to cut four baskets of winter flowers and help hand them out to the people of the town:
   A. Nobody
   B. Claretty Jake
   C. The Lady Mayoress
   D. Mistress Owens

4. How old is Nobody when he first comes to the graveyard?
   A. 15
   B. 6
   C. 1 and a half
   D. less than a year

5. This skill is the ability to disappear and walk unnoticed.
   A. Sliding
   B. Fading
   C. Dreamwalking
   D. Haunting

6. After their first adventure in the Barrow, Scarlett moves to:
   A. London
   B. Ireland
   C. Scotland
   D. America

7. This person's idea of lessons consisted of giving lists which must be memorized.
   A. Silas
   B. Mrs. Owens
   C. Miss Lupescu
   D. Mr. Pennyworth

8. What sort of creatures try to take Bod away to become one of them?
   A. Ghosts
   B. Werewolves
   C. Ghouls
   D. Night-Gaunts

9. Bod ends up in Potter's Field when he:
   A. gets lost and hops on the wrong bus
   B. Falls out of a tree trying to get an apple
   C. Follows a fox through some bushes
   D. Decides to explore a new area of the graveyard

10. How much money does Bod have saved up?
    A. Fifty dollars
    B. Just over 2 pounds
    C. A few pennies
    D. None

11. What does Bod plan to buy for a friend?

    A. Food   B. a coat   C. bus tickets   D. a headstone

12. What does Bod try to sell in order to get enough money for Liza's gift?

    A. his coat   B. an old knife

    C. a brooch from the Barrow   D. Mrs. Owens' jewelry

13. Who saves Bod from the shop where he is imprisoned?

    A. Silas   B. Miss Lupescu   C. Mrs. Owens   D. Liza

14. What book does Nobody "borrow" from another resident of the graveyard who demands it be returned?

    A. *The Bible*   B. *Robinson Crusoe*

    C. *The Cat in the Hat*   D. *War & Peace*

15. Which of the following spirits dances the Macabray with Nobody?

    A. Mrs. Owens   B. Mother Slaughter|

    C. Scarlett   D. Liza

16. Nobody is practically invisible at his school until he does this:

    A. stands up to some bullies

    B. wins a spelling bee

    C. makes the highest grades in the class

    D. corrects his history teacher

17. Who lies to the police in order to get Bod arrested?

    A. Nick   B. Liza   C. Mo   D. Silas

18. Scarlet meets this person the first time she returns to the graveyard after moving back from Scotland.

    A. Bod   B. Mr. Frost   C. Mrs. Owens   D. Silas

19. The first time Scarlett sees Bod after moving back from Scotland is in:

    A. a dream   B. the graveyard   C. a picture   D. the newspaper

20. Silas & Miss Lupescu travel to _____ where they fight against an enemy in some deep caves.

    A. Vladivostock   B. Warsaw   C. London   D. America

21. Scarlett asks this person for help in solving the mystery of the murder of Nobody's family.

    A. her mother   B. a librarian   C. Mr. Frost   D. Mr. Ketch

22. Mr. Frost is taken away to be the new master of what creature?

    A. The Sleer   B. a werewolf   C. the Honour Guard   D. a ghoul

23. At the end of the story, Nobody :

A. settles back into the tomb with his parents

B. becomes a ghoul

C. leaves the graveyard to see the world

D. visits Silas' home

24. One of the first signs that Bod is losing his abilities is that he:

A. sometimes cannot see ghosts

B. can no longer Fade

C. gets locked out of the graveyard

D. hits his head on the ground instead of passing through it

25. This is the only remaining text on Mother Slaughter's headstone.

A. Mother   B. Her   C. Laugh   D. Eliza

Test Question Answer Key:

Character Questions:

1. F
2. D
3. B
4. A
5. C
6. E
7. B
8. E
9. A
10. C
11. F
12. D

Story Questions:

1. B
2. A
3. C
4. C
5. B
6. C
7. C
8. C
9. B
10. B
11. D
12. C
13. D
14. B
15. D
16. A
17. C
18. B
19. A
20. B
21. C
22. A
23. C
24. A
25. C

The Graveyard Book Vocabulary Puzzle
Solve the puzzle, then use the remaining letters to see some advice Mrs. Owens gave to Nobody.

```
W I G H T S O A T N D B T A L Q L E A H
V E N O P B N N O E A N A P A U T H C U
N T A K E O E I T R E D R P F A E O N A
T X U L R M T O R M I O T R F D O E C N
Z C I A A C O O N S V N C O O R Y D O O
M S K M N F W O C I Q L J B B A C I J I
K A R U G I D O D D I S C A R N A T E T
O I S N H N M E B P V G F T J T R R P I
F U O T A F N P Y P R O M I S C U O U S
B R U B I C B O L X S O X O D P D D O O
W B A T E C O M W A E N P N C J B I I P
D R E V E N A N T S C L A I E A O H P M
K D G H O U L T Y C E A P R T T C O S I
E C N E C S E N I M U L B O E I S H H P
S N O I N I M O D N S I A L P T O A E Y
N E V I R H S N U H G D I H E A Q U H D
P I E B A L D I N C O N G R U O U S S Y
J U D D E R E D B A L M I L M T X U U Z
B D O G G E R E L F H T L L E M L L E P
S U R R U S U S L A Y X O M M U L M F R
```

ABANDONMENT	ANORAK	APOPLEXY	APPROBATION
BALM	BARROW	BROOCH	CACHED
DISCARNATE	DISCOMFITED	DOGGEREL	DOMINIONS
FIRMAMENT	GHOUL	HASTEN	IMPLACABLE
IMPOSITION	INCONGRUOUS	JUDDERED	LUMINESCENCE
LUMMOX	MASTICATING	OBDURACY	OBELISK
OFFAL	PELLMELL	PIEBALD	POSTERITY
PROMISCUOUS	PROPITIOUS	PROVIDENCE	
QUADRANT	REVENANTS	SNARE	SUSURRUS
UNCTION	UNSHRIVEN	WIGHTS	WRONGFOOTED

— — — — — — — — — — — — — — — —

The Graveyard Book Rhyming Riddles

The answer to each of the following riddles will be a pair of rhyming words, each having one syllable.

Example: an obese feline
Answer: Fat cat

1. Spittle from the Duke of Westminster— _____ _____

2. Mr. Owens' role when he has company—_____ _____

3. An illness among the dead—_____ _____

4. A soft landing on Carstairs' coffin—_____ _____

5. When Nobody took something from the barrow—_____ _____

6. Jack's statement of purpose— _____ _____

7. Where the Bishop of Bath & wells might be educated—_____ _____

8. A gamble on the Macabray—_____ _____

9. If the man Jack had bad directions—_ _____ _____

10. Someone who pulled jack from Carstairs' grave did this- _____ _____

The Graveyard Book Rhyming Riddles

The answer to each of the following riddles will be a pair of rhyming words, each having one syllable.

Example: an obese feline
Answer: Fat cat

1. Spittle from the Duke of Westminster—   _____ _____

2. Mr. Owens' role when he has company—   _____ _____

3. An illness among the dead—   _____ _____

4. A soft landing on Carstairs' coffin—   _____ _____

5. When Nobody took something from the barrow—   _____ _____

6. Jack's statement of purpose—   _____ _____

7. Where the Bishop of Bath & wells might be educated—_____ _____

8. A gamble on the Macabray—   _____ _____

9. If the man Jack had bad directions—   _____ _____

10. Someone who pulled jack from Carstairs' grave did this- _____ _____

The Graveyard Book Rhyming Riddles (Answer Key)

The answer to each of the following riddles will be a pair of rhyming words, each having one syllable.

Example: an obese feline
Answer: Fat cat

1. Spittle from the Duke of Westminster— Ghoul Drool

2. Mr. Owens' role when he has company— Ghost host

3. An illness among the dead—Wight Blight

4. A soft landing on Carstairs' coffin—Grave save

5. When Nobody took something from the barrow—Brooch Poach

6. Jack's statement of purpose— Will Kill

7. Where the Bishop of Bath & wells might be educated—Ghoul School

8. A gamble on the Macabray—Dance chance

9. If the man Jack had bad directions— Lost Frost

10. Someone who pulled Jack from Carstairs' grave did this- Fetch Ketch

The Graveyard Book
Review Crossword

See how well you remember the characters and events of the novel with this puzzle!

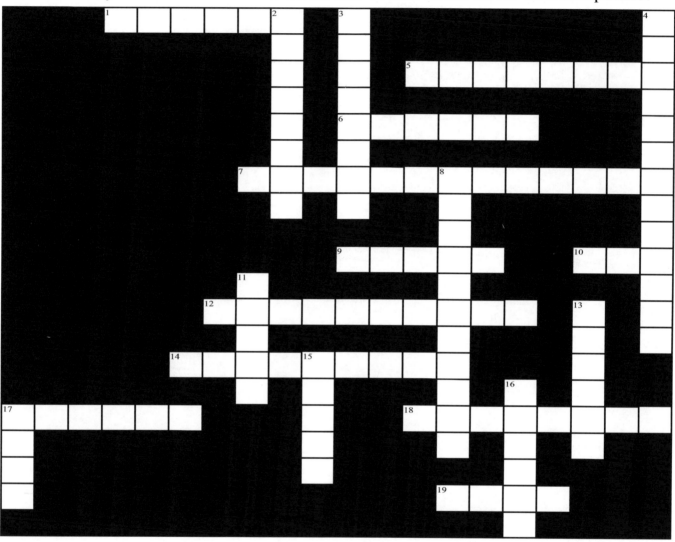

Across

1 The skill of disappearing from people s awareness
5 Where Scarlett moved after she & the boy became friends
6 The last name of the shop owner who traps the boy.
7 The witch buried in the Potters' Field
9 The last name of the man who killed the boy's family
10 What Kandar carried for good luck
12 The flying creature that helps save the boy from the ghouls.
14 The item the boy wants to buy for his friend, Liza.
17 A young boy who is raised by the residents of a graveyard
18 The boy s only living friend
19 The man who killed the boy's family

Down

2 The city with red skies where the ghouls live
3 The dance that the graveyard residents and the people of the town perform together
4 This is the character who convinces the graveyard residents to let the boy stay
8 A werewolf, or "Hound of God" who occasionally watches over the boy.
11 The boy s guardian, he is neither living nor dead
13 What each living person was given on the night they danced with the graveyard residents
15 The creatures who live in the barrow
16 The item the boy steals from the barrow
17 The bully that the boy scares by Dreamwalking.

The Graveyard Book
Review Crossword Answer Key

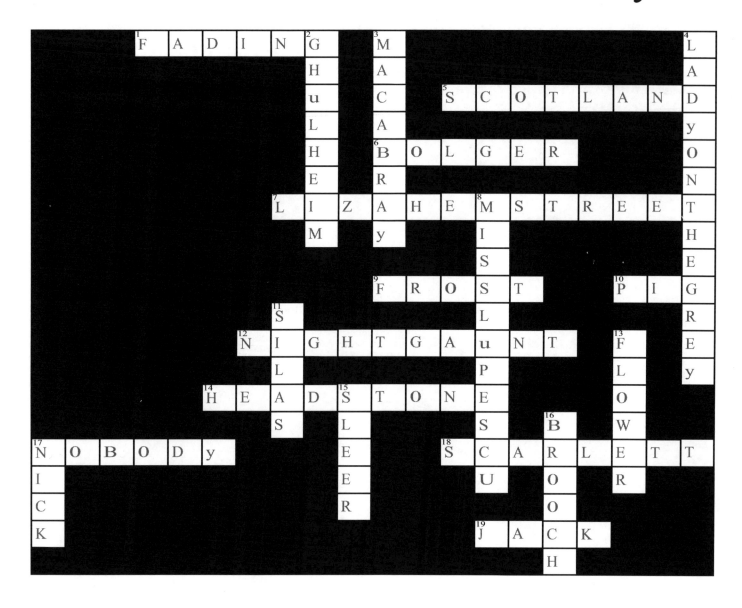

Made in the USA
San Bernardino, CA
17 October 2017